THAT'S NO DiNO!

OR IS IT?

WHAT MAKES A DINOSAUR A DINOSAUR

HELAINE BECKER • MARIE-ÈVE TREMBLAY

Kids Can Press

For my father, Aaron Becker. May his memory be a blessing. — H.B.

To my little Augustine, who let me finish this book on time (almost!). And to David for keeping little Augustine under control (almost!). — M-È.T.

Author's Note

To research this book, I consulted dozens of resources, including monographs, research papers and articles published in scientific journals. I also spoke with paleontologists, including Dr. Scott Persons and Dr. François Therrien (Royal Tyrell Museum), who kindly reviewed the manuscript for accuracy.

Curious readers can refer to some of these documents online. I found the sources listed on page 32 helpful for establishing basic facts and pointing me to further research. Readers should be aware that there is a great deal of misinformation about prehistoric life on the web and should therefore check all sources carefully for scientific legitimacy.

Please note as well that many of the creatures included in this book are known from only a few fossils and are therefore not fully documented, and information about them is difficult to find. New fossils are being found regularly, causing older print works or websites to become dated.

Published in Canada and the U.S. by Kids Can Press Ltd.
25 Dockside Drive, Toronto, ON M5A 0B5

Kids Can Press is a Corus Entertainment Inc. company

www.kidscanpress.com

The artwork in this book was rendered digitally in Photoshop.
The text is set in Absent Grotesque.

Edited by Katie Scott and Kathleen Keenan
Designed by Andrew Dupuis

FSC
MIX
Paper from responsible sources
FSC® C008047

Printed and bound in Shenzhen, China, in 10/2020 by C & C Offset

CM 21 0 9 8 7 6 5 4 3 2 1

Library and Archives Canada Cataloguing in Publication

Title: That's no dino! Or is it?: what makes a dinosaur a dinosaur / written by Helaine Becker ; illustrated by Marie-Ève Tremblay.
Names: Becker, Helaine, author. I
Tremblay, Marie-Ève, illustrator.
Description: Includes index.
Identifiers: Canadiana 20190223391 I ISBN 9781525300233 (hardcover)
Subjects: LCSH: Animals, Fossil — Juvenile literature.
I LCSH: Dinosaurs — Juvenile literature.
Classification: LCC QE765 .B43 2020 I DDC j560 — dc23

Kids Can Press gratefully acknowledges that the land on which our office is located is the traditional territory of many nations, including the Mississaugas of the Credit, the Anishnabeg, the Chippewa, the Haudenosaunee and the Wendat peoples, and is now home to many diverse First Nations, Inuit and Métis peoples.

We thank the Government of Ontario, through Ontario Creates; the Ontario Arts Council; the Canada Council for the Arts; and the Government of Canada for supporting our publishing activity.

What's a Dino, Anyway?

You're probably familiar with lots of dinosaurs, such as *Stegosaurus* or *Triceratops*. You know that they lived a long time ago. But do you know what special traits they all shared? In other words, do you know what made a dinosaur a dinosaur?

As more and more fossils are found, we learn new information about prehistoric beasts. In this book, you'll come face-to-face with many creatures. Some are dinosaurs. Some are less well-known animal species.

You'll find out how scientists decide which animals are dinosaurs and which aren't. And you'll learn one current definition of "dinosaur."

What you discover just might surprise you!

Anomalocaris

(Ah-noh-ma-loh-KAH-riss)

Lived 508 million years ago

Hundreds of millions of years ago, the oceans were full of tiny creatures. When *Anomalocaris* appeared, it seemed gigantic by comparison! Because of its bulk, it needed to eat a lot of itty-bitty creatures to survive. Its huge eyes helped it find prey in the murky water. Then it would seize the prey with its two graspers, shove the food into its mouth and crush it.

    Anomalocaris had a hard shell covering its body instead of a backbone. But **all dinosaurs had a backbone**. *Anomalocaris* was related to today's shrimp, crabs and cockroaches.

Hard exterior shell

Up to 1 m (3.3 ft.) long

AHH!

Huge buggy eyes at the ends of stalks

A pineapple ring-shaped mouth to crush prey

AHH!

WAS IT A DINO?
✗ had a backbone
NOPE! NOT A DINO.

Platyhystrix
(Plat-ee-HISS-tricks)

Lived 299–279.5 million years ago

Box-like skull and frog-like face

Numerous small teeth

About 1 m (3.3 ft.) long

Doesn't *Platyhystrix*'s sail, claws and teeth make it look like a dinosaur? But it wasn't one.

Here's why: *Platyhystrix* probably laid its eggs in water. Also, it probably lived the first part of its life in water and the second part on land. It would have looked very different at each stage of its life, the same way a tadpole looks different from a frog.

Animals such as frogs and *Platyhystrix* that spend time in water and on land are called amphibians.

But **dinosaurs were not amphibians**. They were reptiles. Reptiles have backbones and dry, scaly skin. They also hatch from eggs laid on land and look the same throughout their lives.

Jagged sail on back

Scaly skin

Clawed feet

WAS IT A DINO?
✔ had a backbone
✘ was not an amphibian
NOPE! NOT A DINO.

Elasmotherium

(El-az-moh-THEER-ee-um)

Lived 2.6 million–39 000 years ago

Huge horn on forehead

Muscular body covered with tough, thick skin

Front feet larger than hind feet

Like the well-known dino *Triceratops*, this huge herbivore, or plant-eating animal, had a tough hide. This hide was probably covered in hair that kept *Elasmotherium* warm in the frosty northern areas where it lived.

Also like *Triceratops*, it had an enormous horn. It may have used the horn to defend itself.

So, was *Elasmotherium* a dinosaur like *Triceratops*? Nope! *Elasmotherium* was a mammal. Like almost all mammals (humans included), *Elasmotherium* had hair and nursed its young with milk. **Dinosaurs were not mammals** — remember, they were reptiles.

About 4.5 m (14.8 ft.) long

Shaggy coat

WAS IT A DINO?
- ✔ had a backbone
- ✔ was not an amphibian
- ✘ **was not a mammal**

NOPE! NOT A DINO.

THAT'S NO UNICORN!

A UNICORN!

Dimetrodon

(Die-MEH-troh-don)

Lived 295–272 million years ago

Large sail
on back

DID SOMEBODY SAY DIMO-SAUR?

Sharp, jagged teeth
varying in size

Up to 4.6 m (15.1 ft.) long

Like *Platyhystrix*, *Dimetrodon* had a sail on its back. But unlike *Platyhystrix*, *Dimetrodon* laid its eggs on land, not in water.

Does that make it a dino? Guess again! *Dimetrodon* was a kind of animal called a sphenacodontid (SFEN-uh-coh-DON-tid). Sphenacodontids were similar to modern reptiles, such as lizards and crocodiles, but they had a key difference. Their skulls had a single large hole right behind each eye.

Like today's lizards and crocodiles, **dinosaurs were diapsids**. That means their skulls had *two* holes on each side. One was behind the eye, and the other was on top of the skull. Dinosaurs also had a *third* hole in front of each eye!

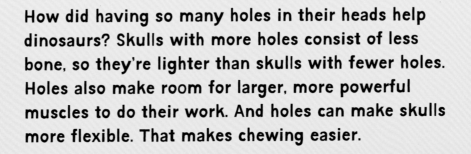

How did having so many holes in their heads help dinosaurs? Skulls with more holes consist of less bone, so they're lighter than skulls with fewer holes. Holes also make room for larger, more powerful muscles to do their work. And holes can make skulls more flexible. That makes chewing easier.

Long tail

WAS IT A DINO?
✔ had a backbone
✔ was not an amphibian
✔ was not a mammal
✘ **was a diapsid**
NOPE! NOT A DINO.

Protorosaurus
(Pro-toh-ruh-SORE-us)

Lived 260–251 million years ago

Protorosaurus was a reptile that lived more than 250 million years ago. It had a long neck that may have helped it reach leaves and other hard-to-reach tasty tidbits. It probably ate insects, too.

Some dinosaurs had long necks, but *Protorosaurus* wasn't a dinosaur. **Dinosaurs lived during the Mesozoic era**, about 251 to 66 million years ago. *Protorosaurus* lived millions of years before that. The group of animals it belongs to included dinosaurs' ancestors, plus the ancestors of other reptiles, such as modern crocodiles.

Up to 2.5 m (8.2 ft.) long

Long tail

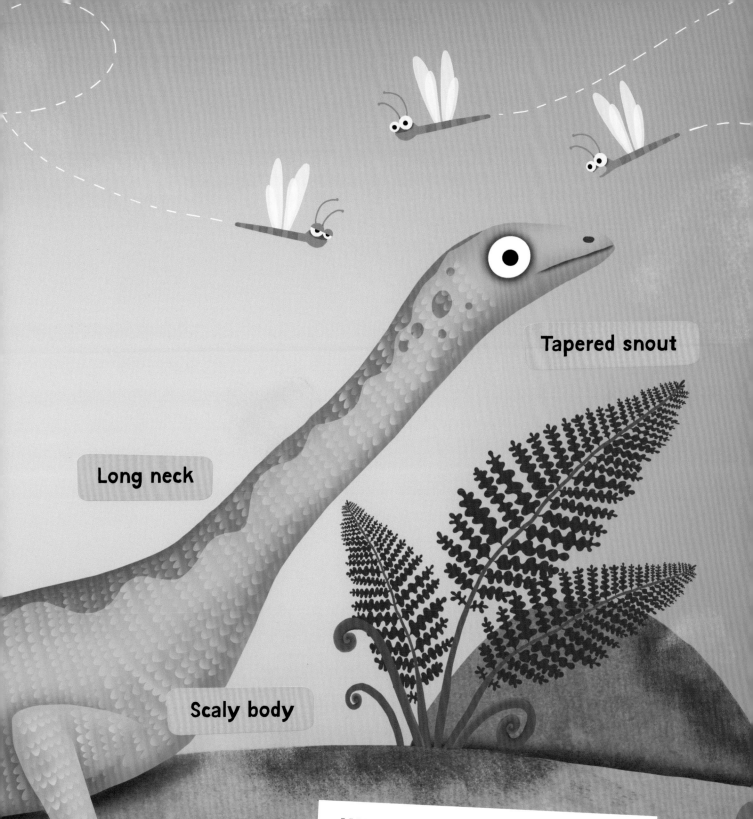

Tapered snout

Long neck

Scaly body

WAS IT A DINO?
- ✔ had a backbone
- ✔ was not an amphibian
- ✔ was not a mammal
- ✔ was a diapsid
- ✗ lived during the Mesozoic era

NOPE! NOT A DINO.

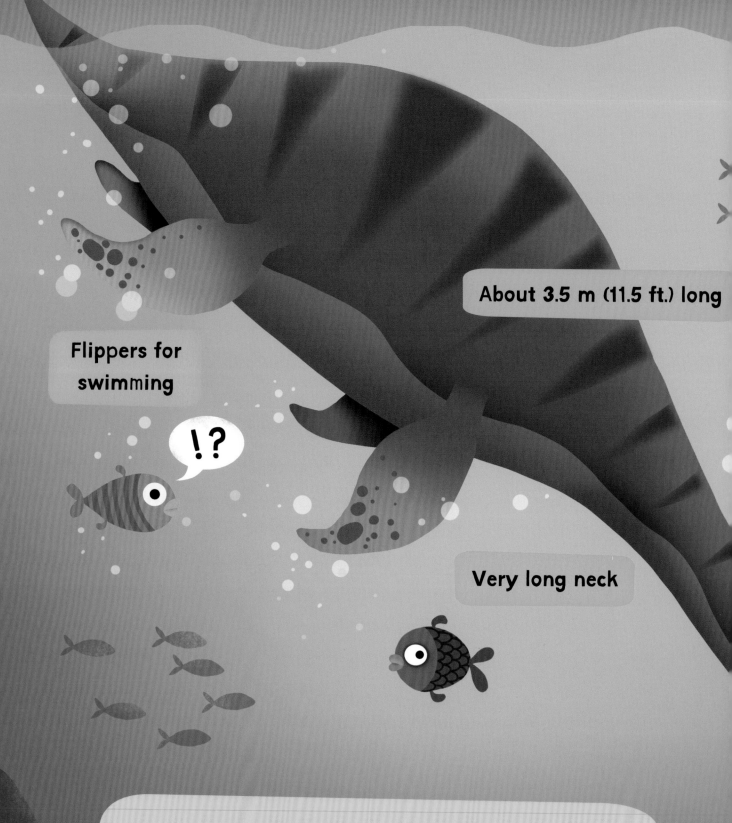

About 3.5 m (11.5 ft.) long

Flippers for swimming

⁉

Very long neck

Like most modern land animals, most dinosaurs were probably able to swim short distances. Some fish-eating dinosaurs, such as *Spinosaurus* and *Baryonyx*, likely spent a lot of time in the water, just like modern crocodiles. But no known dinosaurs lived their lives entirely in water.

Plesiosaurus
(Pleh-zee-oh-SORE-us)

Lived 199.6–175.6 million years ago

If you were a fish, you would not have wanted to meet *Plesiosaurus*! It used its extra-long neck to strike at prey from a distance. Then, its mouth full of sharp teeth could hold the wriggling prey tight. Strong, stiff paddle-like limbs helped *Plesiosaurus* cruise smoothly through the water in search of its next meal.

Plesiosaurus was a diapsid reptile. It even lived during the Mesozoic era. But was it a dinosaur?

No. *Plesiosaurus* called the ocean its home. Several dinosaurs were excellent swimmers, but no species of dinosaur lived in the water all the time. **Dinosaurs were land animals.**

Small head

!?

WAS IT A DINO?
- ✔ had a backbone
- ✔ was not an amphibian
- ✔ was not a mammal
- ✔ was a diapsid
- ✔ lived during the Mesozoic era
- ✘ **was a land animal**

NOPE! NOT A DINO.

Huge, leathery wings spanning
up to 11 m (36 ft.)

Spindly
hind legs

Very muscular
front legs

Quetzalcoatlus
(KWEH-tzul-coh-AT-lus)

Lived 70–65 million years ago

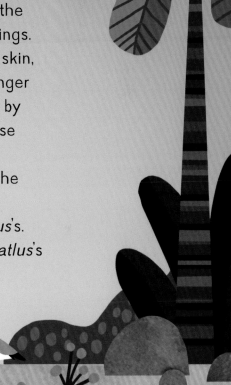

Sharp, toothless beak

Imagine the terrifying sight of gigantic *Quetzalcoatlus* soaring overhead. Its wings were three times longer than those of the wandering albatross, today's flying bird with the longest wings.

Quetzalcoatlus had bat-like wings made up of leathery skin, tough fibers and powerful muscles attached to one long finger on each of its sides. This reptile may have gotten airborne by jumping into the air, propelled by its strong front legs. Those huge wings let it glide great distances.

But **most dinosaurs didn't have bat-like wings**. The wings of all known flying dinosaurs had many fingers and feathers, plus a very different structure than *Quetzalcoatlus*'s. Dinosaurs' bones also had several features that *Quetzalcoatlus*'s bones didn't.

One group of dinosaurs did have bat-like wings: the scansoriopterygids (SCAN-sore-ee-OP-ter-ih-jid). One of these dinosaurs, *Yi qi*, was even given a name that means "strange wings"! But scansoriopterygids had feathers, just like other dinos, and their wings extended from several long fingers, not just one.

WAS IT A DINO?
- ✔ had a backbone
- ✔ was not an amphibian
- ✔ was not a mammal
- ✔ was a diapsid
- ✔ lived during the Mesozoic era
- ✔ was a land animal
- ✘ **didn't have bat-like wings**

NOPE! NOT A DINO.

Teraterpeton
(Teh-ra-**TER**-peh-ton)

Lived 235–228 million years ago

Crocodile-like body

Up to 1.2 m (3.9 ft.) long

Legs splayed out to the side

The name *Teraterpeton* means "wonderful creeping thing." This reptile was wonderful ... and weird! It had a stretched-out face, big eyes and lots of little teeth at the back of its mouth. It looked like a cross between a bird and a crocodile. And just like a crocodile, *Teraterpeton* had a low-slung body, with legs that splayed out to the side.

Dinosaurs didn't have splayed legs like that, though. **Dinosaurs had an upright stance**, with legs that were directly under their bodies. So wonderful creeping *Teraterpeton* was not a dinosaur.

Long, pointy face

Small teeth at back of jaw

ME? A DINO? I'M A STRETCH!

Splayed
(Teraterpeton)

Upright
(dinosaurs)

WAS IT A DINO?
- ✔ had a backbone
- ✔ was not an amphibian
- ✔ was not a mammal
- ✔ was a diapsid
- ✔ lived during the Mesozoic era
- ✔ was a land animal
- ✔ didn't have bat-like wings
- ✘ **had an upright stance**

NOPE! NOT A DINO.

Poposaurus
(Pop-uh-SORE-us)

Lived 237–201.3 million years ago

EVEN MY FOSSILS SAY I'M HIP.

About 4 m (13.1 ft.) long

Small teeth at back of jaw

Upright stance

Front limbs much shorter than hind limbs

Claws on front "hands"

Poposaurus was a fearsome predator. Thanks to its upright stance, it could lift its upper body and walk or run fast on two legs. *Poposaurus* could easily run down speedy prey and rip them open with its razor-sharp teeth.

Many dinos ran fast on two legs. But was *Poposaurus* a dino? No. The bones of its pelvis reveal why. Many animals, including *Poposaurus*, have a layer of bone inside their hip sockets — the spaces where their leg bones fit into their pelvises. Animals without that bone layer have what are called "complete holes" where their leg bones fit in. Fossils show that **dinosaurs had complete holes in their pelvises**.

Walked and ran on two legs (bipedal)

WAS IT A DINO?
- ✔ had a backbone
- ✔ was not an amphibian
- ✔ was not a mammal
- ✔ was a diapsid
- ✔ lived during the Mesozoic era
- ✔ was a land animal
- ✔ didn't have bat-like wings
- ✔ had an upright stance
- ✗ **had complete holes in pelvis**

NOPE! NOT A DINO.

Sacisaurus

(Sah-see-SORE-us)

I'M NO DINO?

Lived 228–208.5 million years ago

Tiny teeth

Up to 1.5 m (4.9 ft.) long

Strong legs

Extra-long
hind limbs

Sacisaurus certainly looked like a dinosaur. It lived on land in the right time period and had an upright stance. In fact, it had every dinosaur trait — except one!

Dinosaurs' ancestors had hands with flexible front fingers and a specific number of bones. These hands were able to grasp things the way human hands can. Over hundreds of thousands of years, some dinosaur species lost this ability because their bones fused together. But all dinosaur fossils share the same basic hand anatomy, or structure, so we know that **dinosaurs had grasping hands**.

Sacisaurus's front claws probably didn't have that same anatomy. Scientists think it belonged to a group of animals that were not dinos. No *Sacisaurus* hand fossils have been found, so we can't say for sure. But if it's true, *Sacisaurus* was very similar to dinosaurs … but was not a dinosaur.

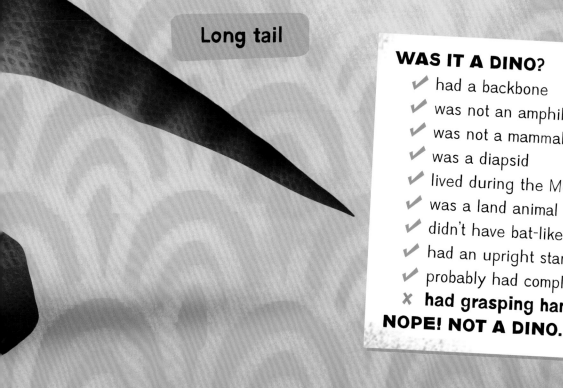

Long tail

WAS IT A DINO?
- ✔ had a backbone
- ✔ was not an amphibian
- ✔ was not a mammal
- ✔ was a diapsid
- ✔ lived during the Mesozoic era
- ✔ was a land animal
- ✔ didn't have bat-like wings
- ✔ had an upright stance
- ✔ probably had complete holes in pelvis
- ✘ **had grasping hands**

NOPE! NOT A DINO.

Velociraptor
(Veh-lah-sih-RAP-tor)

Lived 75–71 million years ago

Feathered

Bipedal

Claws on hind feet

It was fast. It was smart. It was a fearsome Mesozoic era reptile that could run on two upright legs and grip prey in its front claws. Was *Velociraptor* really a dino? Yes!

Meat-eating *Velociraptor* fed on other dinos, such as *Protoceratops*. Its greatest weapon was a sharp claw on each of its hind feet that it could use like a dagger. *Velociraptor* also had feathers, which might have attracted mates or kept this dino warm.

About 1.8 m (5.9 ft.) from skull to tail

Sharp teeth for tearing meat

Front claws for grasping

WAS IT A DINO?
- ✔ had a backbone
- ✔ was not an amphibian
- ✔ was not a mammal
- ✔ was a diapsid
- ✔ lived during the Mesozoic era
- ✔ was a land animal
- ✔ didn't have bat-like wings
- ✔ had an upright stance
- ✔ had complete holes in pelvis
- ✔ had grasping hands

YUP! IT'S A DINO.

It's one of the most famous dinosaurs in the world. But wait — *T. rex* wasn't very good at grasping things. How, then, can *Tyrannosaurus rex* still be considered a dinosaur?

By examining many fossils, paleontologists (the scientists who study dinosaurs) determined that *T. rex*'s ancestors *did* have grasping ability. The species gradually evolved (changed over time) and lost it! Because of its history, *T. rex* still gets a dinosaur thumbs-up.

More True Dinosaurs

No one knows for sure how many different kinds of dinosaurs once roamed the planet. Fossils are hard to find and even harder to identify. Today, more than 700 dinosaur species have been identified, and more fossils are being discovered all the time.

Whatever the number, paleontologists *do* know that dinosaurs dominated the planet for around 165 million years. They did so by adapting to different environmental conditions. Some, such as *Spinosaurus*, became fierce meat-eating predators, while others, such as *Parasaurolophus*, grazed on plants. Some grew ginormous, such as *Argentinosaurus* — it weighed in at 70 t (77 tons), the weight of more than 12 adult male African elephants! Others, such as *Compsognathus*, shrank to the size of a crow.

Parasaurolophus

Spinosaurus

Compsognathus

Argentinosaurus

Chicken-a-saurus?

Dinosaurs are supposed to be extinct. But there *are* animals alive today that have almost all of the dinosaur characteristics you've learned about, including backbones, grasping hands and upright stances. They're diapsid land animals. And they're not mammals or amphibians ... they're birds. So does that mean a chicken is a dinosaur? Dino experts say yes!

Like *T. rex*, birds have 100 percent dinosaur ancestors. And like *T. rex*, they have every accepted dinosaur trait, or variations of these traits that evolved from the original dinosaur version. For example, birds once had complete holes in their hips that eventually closed up.

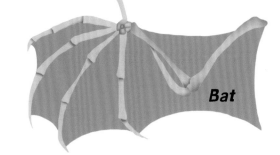

Bat

Bird

Scientists also think that birds once had fingers that became feathered wings. These strong, warm wings would have allowed birds to survive tough times while traveling long distances to find food. These adaptations may have helped birds avoid extinction and survive past the Mesozoic era and into modern times — unlike other dinosaurs.

Scientists now agree that all avians, or birds, are species of dinosaurs. Yep, that includes chickens! Birds are the only branch of the dinosaur family that lives today. Extinct dinosaurs are now more accurately called non-avian dinosaurs.

The many different kinds of dinosaurs are usually divided into two groups: the saurischians (meaning "reptile-hipped") and the ornithischians (meaning "bird-hipped"). The names come from the way the dinosaurs' pelvic bones are shaped. As scientists discover more fossils and learn more about dinosaur evolution, these groupings may change.

The Saurischians

There are two main groups of saurischian dinosaurs. One is the sauropodomorphs. They were herbivores, or plant eaters. Most were quadrupedal, which means they had four feet.

Patagotitan

Saurischians's pelvises

Tyrannosaurus rex

The other group is the theropods, which were bipedal, or two-legged. Some were herbivores, but many more, such as *T. rex*, *Allosaurus* and *Ceratosaurus*, were carnivores, or meat eaters.

The Ornithischians

Dinosaurs you probably recognize, such as *Stegosaurus* and *Triceratops*, were ornithischians.

Stegosaurus

Ornithischians's pelvises

There were also some less well-known ornithischians, such as *Tenontosaurus* and *Pachycephalosaurus*. All ornithischians were herbivores.

Pachycephalosaurus

Conclusion

Dinosaurs are just one type of extinct animal from prehistoric times. You've learned about many others in this book. Many species survived for hundreds of thousands of years until changing environmental conditions and increased competition for food caused them to die out. New species arose to take their place.

Until recently, scientists thought all dinosaurs went extinct 65 million years ago. But now, thanks to the discovery of new fossils, we know that some of the dinosaurs evolved into birds. Today, these dinosaur descendants still live and thrive ... right outside your window!

One current definition of *dinosaur* might look like this:

- ✔ has a backbone
- ✔ is not an amphibian
- ✔ is not a mammal
- ✔ is a diapsid + has an extra third hole in each side of the skull
- ✔ lived from the Mesozoic era **until the present time**
- ✔ is a land mammal
- ✔ doesn't have **featherless** bat-like wings
- ✔ has an upright stance
- ✔ has complete holes in pelvis, **or has a pelvis that evolved from one with holes**
- ✔ has grasping hands **or features, such as feathered wings, that evolved from hands**

Will birds take over Earth one day by outcompeting other successful species, like (gulp!) us? Only time will tell.

Glossary

amphibian: a cold-blooded animal, such as a frog, that spends the first part of its life in water, breathing through gills, and its adulthood on land, breathing with lungs

anatomy: the shape and structure of a living thing's body

ancestor: a direct relative that lived long ago

avian: like a bird. *Non-avian* means not like a bird.

bipedal: able to walk on two legs

carnivore: an animal that eats meat, meaning other animals

descend: in life science, the way modern species originated by evolving from earlier ancestors

diapsid: having two pairs of holes in the skull

evolution: the process by which all living creatures change, or adapt, over long periods of time to survive. Eventually, if there are many changes, an animal's or plant's descendants will become a new species.

extinction: when there are no more individuals of a species alive anywhere in the world. These species are said to be extinct, or to have died out.

fossil: an impression of a past living creature left in rock

herbivore: an animal that eats plants

mammal: an animal, such as a human, that has hair and nurses its young with milk

ornithischian (bird-hipped): a type of dinosaur with a pelvis that resembles a bird's pelvis

paleontologist: a scientist who studies ancient life, including dinosaurs, by looking at fossils

pelvis: the part of the skeleton that connects the legs to the spine

predator: a creature that hunts and kills other animals for food

prehistoric: existing in ancient times, before written records

prey: a creature that is hunted for food by a predator

quadrupedal: able to walk on four legs

reptile: an animal, such as a crocodile, that has dry, leathery skin and lays soft-shelled eggs on land

saurischian (reptile-hipped): a type of dinosaur with a pelvis that resembles a reptile's pelvis

sauropodomorph: a type of saurischian dinosaur, such as *Brachiosaurus* and *Apatosaurus*, that ate plants and had four feet and a long neck and tail

scansoriopterygid: a group of small dinosaurs that were able to glide on bat-like wings

species: a group of living things that have characteristics in common and can breed with one another to produce a new generation

sphenacodontid: a kind of animal with both mammalian and reptilian characteristics that lived long before the dinosaurs

theropod: a group of saurischian dinosaurs, such as *T. rex*, that walked on two legs and ate mostly meat

Index

Selected Sources

Websites

https://dkfindout.com/us/dinosaurs-and-prehistoric-life/
https://fossilhunters.xyz/defining-dinosaurs/axial-bones-of-a-dinosaur-hips-backbone-tail-and-ribs.html
https://britannica.com/animal/dinosaur
https://ucmp.berkeley.edu/taxa/verts/diapsida.php

Books

Becker, Helaine. *Megabugs: And Other Prehistoric Critters That Roamed the Planet.* Illustrated by John Bindon. Toronto: Kids Can Press, 2019.

The Dinosaur Book. New York: DK Publishing, 2018.

Dinosaur!: Dinosaurs and Other Amazing Prehistoric Creatures as You've Never Seen Them Before. New York: DK Publishing, 2014.

Dupont, Clémence. *A Brief History of Life on Earth.* New York: Prestel Publishing, 2019.

Lendler, Ian. *The First Dinosaur: How Science Solved the Greatest Mystery on Earth.* Illustrated by C. M. Butzer. New York: Margaret K. McElderry Books, 2019.

National Museum of Natural History and Blake Edgar. *Smithsonian Dinosaurs and Other Amazing Creatures from Deep Time.* Washington, D.C.: Smithsonian Books, 2019.

Rake, Matthew. *Prehistoric Sea Beasts.* Illustrated by Simon Mendez. Minneapolis: Lerner Publishing Group, 2017.

Sewell, Matt. *Forgotten Beasts: Amazing Creatures That Once Roamed the Earth.* London: Pavilion Children's, 2019.